THE SHOEMAKER'S WIFE

and other poems

THE SHOEMAKER'S WIFE

and other poems

LOTTE KRAMER

HIPPOPOTAMUS PRESS

ACKNOWLEDGEMENTS are due to the editors of the following publications *Agenda, Argo, Ariel, Candelabrum, Chapman, Christian Science Monitor, Country Life, Countryman, Cyphers, Double Space, Encounter, European Judaism, Jewish Chronicle, Jewish Quarterly, Literary Review, New Statesman, 'No Holds Barred' (Women's Press), Ore, Other Poetry, Outposts, The Pen, Poetry Durham, Samphire, Tribune, Ver Poets, Writing Women.*

First published 1987
by HIPPOPOTAMUS PRESS
26 Cedar Road, Sutton, Surrey

British Library Cataloguing in Publication Data
Kramer, Lotte
The Shoemaker's Wife and other poems.
I. Title
821'.914 PR6061.R3/

ISBNO-904179-35-4
ISBNO-904179-36-2 Pbk

Cover design by B. S. Andrews
based, on the painting *Schusterwerkstatt*
by Max Liebermann

*Ten copies only of the cloth edition have
been numbered and signed by the author*

Printed in Great Britain
by The September Press, Wellingborough, Northants

CONTENTS

FORE.S.

Scholars passed by a dead dog. The disciples said: "How awful its smell!" Their master said: "How white its teeth!"

Bachya Ibn Pakuda *(circa* 1050-1120)

I

ARRIVAL

When I arrived
The gate was always open,
Broad and unhinged,
The gravel underfoot
Pale apricot,
And in the house itself
The air was bright
At first. A generous
Untidiness
Past sideboards, chairs,
And tables where
So many hands had met,
Until a step, a stair, led
Unexpectedly
Into a darkness which the day
Could never sear:
Those anterooms, mysterious
Passages,
The storing corners by
A spiral stair
Held more than dust. For years
I smelt and saw them
Only in disguise.

So here was England:
By the fire-place,
The tea with scones and soda-bread,
The Irish voice
That read from Dickens, made
Him live for us;
The passion in each breath,
Her Schubert songs!
The shabby, shaking figure
Who was once an

Indian Army Colonel,
Now absorbed in roses, lawns,
And the same curry every week.
A portrait hung
Large, on her study wall:
A grandmother
From Java – beautiful
And like the rest:
A contradiction
Of this island universe.
And not one door was ever locked.

AT DOVER HARBOUR

Behind this rough sleeve of water
There lies the heart's island, set in
A harvest of stone, its work done.

Ahead, the broad hand of Europe
Opens her lined landscape, the skin
Hard and calloused with bitter blood.

And the arm heaves under grey cloth
Releasing the split signal of
The lighthouse of love with its white

Exploding star, turning always
In the black wind that calls me back
To whispering benedictions.

COVENANT AND GENES

Passing the mirror in the hall
I catch my sudden face
And, startled, see an aunt,
My grandmother, stare back.

Then, as I pay the milkman,
Count the change, they reappear:
White-haired and solid as that
Frail split-second showed.

Shall we become the slaves
Or instruments to ancestors?
Or are they blessing us in these
Incipient moments of redress

When we, perhaps forgetting
Who we are, mix blood
Like dice to empty out
Their numbered, winning days.

CHERRIES

These cherries taste of summer streets to school,
Or rather of the walk there in the heat
When stumbling over melting tar the mile
Seemed endless. Pennies in my fist, the treat

Of shiny cherries waited. The corner
Shop was rich with fruit, all ripening juices
Cased in bumper beads from black to red, more
Like a feast of pregnant marbles than these

Perishable sights. I bought and clutched them
In a coarse brown paper bag. At the first
Break, their squashy sweetness shared our game:
We stained our faces, ears, our frocks, with thirst

For them, ignoring maggots that could lurk
Inside their flesh, a white curl in the dark.

GERMANY 1933

The air was dank with fifty little girls.
Spell-bound they listened to their teacher's tale
Of one young martyr*, one who gave the name
To that new hymn. They wept for him. He burnt

An early hero into ready minds.
And then the oath – they hardly knew what for –
Of loyalty to him whose massive roar
Bludgeoned their ears. There was no choice, no sign

Of something sinister. They longed to serve,
To sing in great processions, hold a flag,
And feel secure under this pagan tag.
A slag-heap waiting for a willing herd.

   'Now choose the one to lead, to march ahead,
    To keep your trust, unfurl the swastika.'
The teacher urged a ballot on the class.
   'The one you like the most' he archly said.

The children chose and named a jewish child.

Horst Wessel

THE SHOEMAKER'S WIFE

She came to us walking, at night.
Our bundle of mended shoes
Hot secrets in her shopping bag.

By the door in the hall she stood
And cried. Her autumn hair
Wild from the wind.

Her red-blue eyes like
Sores in her face,
Sad postmarks

From the cobbler's shop
In the narrow old town
Where her husband hammered

And stitched his days;
Where the sign 'No Jews'
Newly pinned to the door

Pleased her sons'
Keen suspicion
That mastered all our lives.

MEMOIR

On certain days
There would appear a photograph:
A young and handsome officer,
Austro-Hungarian, on her desk.
   'The one I should have married'
She explained 'he fell in the Great War.'
And next to him herself,
A soul-struck girl with eyes of coal.

At other times
A former pupil took his place:
A Leonardo face, lost to her now
In war-anaemic Hertfordshire
Here, she worked hard at living
On the land, at keeping rabbits,
Pigs, at unforgetting.
Her hands were sick with unborn music.

ON SHUTTING THE DOOR

Often, when I leave home,
I think of you,
How you'd have shut the door
That last time
They fetched you out at dawn.

What fears would prophesy,
What intimations
Could foretell the terrors
Of those plains,
The herding into ash?

Or maybe, you looked round
As if before
A holiday, leaving
No trace of dust,
No crumbs for pests, no moths

In cupboards, carpets;
Covered the chairs,
The settee from the glare
Of light and sun,
Turned off the water, gas . . .

NEIGHBOURS 1942-43

So this was how they went:
With layers of clothes
Prepared for ice.
Some gems and coins
Sown into hems,
Perhaps to help escape.

You came the night before
To stem their dark.
To lay your words
On open souls
And bind with hands
A will to outlive hell.

But when your husband fell
In Warsaw's fight,
Left fatherless
Your child – quite close
To him they lost
That breath that willed my life.

LIFT BOY – MARSEILLES 1940-45

From gunning fence
He crawled to woods,
All senses taut.

Alone – as food
Wild berries, leaves
Were stooping warmth.

Always brooding
For wife and son
Tore his breathing.

When snow laced sun
He braved the town,
Laughter and pain.

He feigned a found
Silence. Closed flood
Of ears and tongue:

Unspoken thuds
Of years. His voice
Forgotten. Mud

Pushed into noise
Peopled a cell
Of pending life.

When freedom fell
He hardly knew
His name or choice.

TWO BOYS 1940-44

Two boys played on a farm in France.
Quite ordinary boys. 'No harm
Will touch them', so the farmer priced
His promise for a bar of gold.
He stored and fathered orphaned lives.

Before their bones had stretched full size
Their minds were strung with adult ache.
In earnest they played 'Blind Man's Buff'
Or 'Hide and Seek'. They knew the ways
Of tunnelled moles and fumbling bats.

Their growing pains had hostile names.
Their town-hands learned to crumble soil,
To master trees, to sweat with fear.
We thought them safely caged in barns.
What made him break their padlocked years?

To let the hunter grab his prey
And shunt them on an eastern train
In cattle-trucks to nameless graves
Where fathers never heard them groan:
Amen – for their dumb growing pains.

How did he plough his land and reap
With children's ghosts, their splintered nails,
How did he clean his grubby skin
From their cold questions in its cracks
And shrug away his ailing sin?

CROSSING FRONTIERS

i.m. Paul Wertheimer

We were the black-out dancers
While you lay
Dumb-huddled in dark cellars,
And we ate
Our wholesome war-time rations
While you scraped
The earth for stale compassions:
Empty plates,
The odd potatoes, apples,
And the spate
In fear dug your possessions,
Hoarded hate.

Once, twenty years before then,
You had worn
A young boy's emblem – field-grey
Uniform.
But comrades turned to envy,
Roots were torn.
You crossed the bridge. The Rhine fenced
All their scorn,
Or flooded a new tempest,
Shone to warn
Of devil's marching kinsmen,
Power-borne.

They shelled and spat their twisted
Creed. You fled.
A soldier's cap insisted
On the bed
Of your adoption; listed
Sand and lead:

The Foreign Legion's fisted
Craze instead. –
And still we danced in glibness
While you met
Defeat, hurt faces, misted
Friends as dead.

A tacit town-clerk's warning
Packed your sack.
Your wife and children's practice
Dodged goose-step,
A colonnade of unhinged
Hikers led
By your great courage, clinging
To snow-wet
Rough mountains. Sudden screaming
Halted yet
All freedom in your lifting
Arms, and bled.

THERE

In that street it was always summer;
Hot enough to sit on slabs
Of paving stones, watch grown-ups pass,
Be recognised as my mother's daughter.

There was the tall doorway which led
Through chill darkness into the yard
Where a dung-heap blossomed
In competition with geraniums;

Where the butcher-boy sang as he scoured
A stable or laughingly lassoed
A rope of intestines above his head;
A goat's white kick sharpening the air.

An earth world so divorced
From school and town, from elegance
Partitioning the year's performance,
But warm and sweet as my aunt's yeast buns.

UNCLE JULIUS

Uncle Julius, Jussl for short,
Pulled his pale years
On his early grey head.

Not for him, the Kaiser's framed name
Proudly displayed
On the sitting room wall:

Signature to his young brother's war.
Nor the blade-brains
Of the third one's steep slog

Marching him daily five miles to the town:
Grammar school scholar
Shining the widowhood of their mother.

But Jussl was kind, slow perhaps,
Trundling his textiles through heat and frost,
Tramping about in his brother's old suits.

Not prepared for what was in store.
Not a fighter but praying all night:
Led on a lead through the village street.

AUNT ELISE

My aunt Elise,
Daughter and sister of rabbis,
Was roundness incarnate.

Dripping with long-fringed shawl
And smelling of soap,
Of wax and wood,

She stood with the heat
In a low-beamed room
Of the black and white house:

The mothball wife
Pregnant with prayer
She curled her hands

And widened her eyes
Like frightened pennies:
Questioning her childlessness.

CANTOR

I

A little man
Who sang and wept his chant
In true talmudic fashion,
Standing before
The altar, soapy-voiced,
Swaying his frame in prayer shawl.

He lectured us,
Rather he tried to teach
Divinity to wandering ears,
Instil some spark,
Some reverence in fidget minds
Who mocked his mitred vowels cruelly.

II

The burnt-out school
And synagogue rescued him
To the USA where none
Would use his voice,
His Charlie Chaplin stature
Piously. No bread in his old tune.

Instead he found
His hands, those winter-faced
Keen instruments of gestured life
Gentled a craft:
Repaired, restored antiques.
Oceans away from cassock, shawl.

CHANT OF A RETURN VISIT

Hour after hour the day takes its toll:
I walk where I played, where I learnt the first
Singing, heard the alphabet dancing.

Tramlines still snaking through narrow streets,
Market women with expressionist stalls
Splashing their speech over pot-pourri smells.

I stand by the grass with the cited stone,
By the oposite house where the window speaks
Of the child inside and the burning night.

And behind the white wall: the drone, the drone,
Of the ancient chant that I dare not hear,
Where new faces peer over prayers that weep

Telling of other walls crumbling: 'Oh hear,
Oh Israel hear! Our God is One, is King!'
But the child cannot go where the woman stands.

She walks to the Rhine, to its clear refrain
From the time of her birth to this day that is old
With tunes of eyes, asphalt and stone.

SCHULS TARASP REVISITED

(for my father)

Dear marching hero, tracing your long strides
Along the boulders of the river Inn
Walking away the demons of your mind,
I feel their tremor on the bridge and run

When crossing to the gorge. You loved that Spa:
The elegance beside the steaming spring,
The promenading while you sipped that raw
And sulphurous drink, the afternoons that cling
To Kurhaus gardens, coffee, schmalzy dance,

Light years away from hostile marching songs.
They cushioned you, those quiet weeks, the rhythm
Reeking of Edwardian follies and their time
(And yet between two 20th century wars)
When mountains could displace that crooked cross.

No premonition then of that dark curse
That would destroy your summers, seal my loss.

TRADITION

We have lost the ecstasy of the law,
The word's bindweed;

The sanctity of remembrance has become
A pipeline we measure at intervals,

And the old chant, the white
Sap of ancestors,

Is now a sad tune
Touching the spine in recognition.

NON SEQUITUR

He won't accept
That she can't walk again.
His eighty Polish
Years have only known
Survival, at a cost.
Defeat has no space
In his alphabet.
His blue eyes stare out
Any death.
He burnt out loss with life.

But now he hears
And sees her harsh decline,
And not one comma
Of his bullying love
Can force and free
Her paralysing bones.
Aside, she whispers:
'Ich bin lebensmüd'*.
His ostrich feathers
Tremble in the wind.

* 'I'm tired of living'

FOR FRIEDRICH SANDELS

(March 14 1889–August 5 1984)

> . . . *'Immerhin! Mich wird umgeben*
> *Gotteshimmel dort wie hier,*
> *Und als Totenlampen schweben*
> *Nachts die Sterne über mir.'*
>
> Heinrich Heine, 'WO?'

I

Today I walked in his flat birth country;
The soil still sandy, the Rhine massive.
Born in that corner of the river's knee
He was rooted in a delta of vines,
Could reach out in safety for mountains and seas,
Know and teach many legends and lives.
His creed was Greece, his voice was German.

He straddled the Kaiser's field-grey years.
Then clarity purged each failed decade.
His oracle told of the blackest sights
Which no one believed, no one would fear
Until his Delphic burden proved true.

II

On the day of the burning school
He came walking towards us,
Face as grey as his flapping coat:

'Children' he said
'Our headmaster is dead.
   His house in splinters,
   His room full of gas.

   They only smashed my records.'

III

He was forest and meadows,
River and Lieder,
Would praise the grace
Of the poem, the word.
The bright spine of language
Brought yeast to his blood.
History moved
As water's kinship
Leading us through
Odyssian journeys.
He taught us to weep
With Antigone's pleading
Where law was compassion,
Was courage and love.

IV

'Weep for his passing,
Sing for his living,
Give thanks for the seed
Of his harvest words.'

V

'Justus', his nickname, honoured him.
A celebration of his fair concern
For justice, law and discipline.

We could accept his code of decency,
Learn to respect another's private sphere
And all that forms a friend's identity.

Later, when a new country claimed his word
Of different subjects, languages and creeds,
He marched for civil rights among the crowd.

His Europe changed, became a holiday
Where peaks were climbed by cable-cars, not sweat,
And where a boy's Greek grammar made him cry.

Still anxious in his ninth decade
His letters emphasized his mind's great zest
Probing into and through each complex world.

The day the message came that he had died
I spent in making bread, in kneading dough.
His presence in this ritual close at hand.

DREAMS

You asked me: 'Do you dream?'
Too quickly I agreed.
But then pleaded forgetfulness.

Because there is this ruthlessness in dreams:
I see the queues of death,
Their last relentless walk.

I run and run and run
But never reach them.
Then I fall.

Sometimes you stand there
In the distance,
Arms apart.

Again I run
Into that lean, far light,
But fall outside myself.

II

CIRCUS FIRE

Only a bus-full
Of wire and mud,

Singed blackness
Where hair and skin

Had housed flesh,
Blood and bones.

The rhythm of beaks,
Of quick-eyed feathers

A teaspoon of cinders;
Serpentine reptiles

A chaos of cogwheels.
But unprepared

For human eyes:
In pairs, embracing,

The remnants of apes.

VISIT

In May she knew
These were the steep
Hours of her dying.

By her bedside
We talked of apples
We would pick
In her orchard
In the autumn,

Legitimate lies
Fighting cold vertigo;
We need that solace
To see us through
Her intelligent presence.

TWICE BEREAVED

For her
That was the worst betrayal
After his dying, his decline,
To know he talked of God.

Not of
The Jesus of his childhood
Were his words, no mother's tales,
But parables of prophets

Filled his
Mind, of Palestine, the Old
Testament. Deep in those
Mysteries he battled for

A way
Back to some undergrowth
She'd never heard him mention,
For all their married life was

Orthodox
In unbelief. And so, he left her
Twice bereaved for something
Other, unexplained.

'SOLITUDE' (Marc Chagall, 1933)

The angel soul,
White in its scissored wings,
Flies cradled in blue sky,

While the dark
Weight of fire-clouds
Pours ash on the small town.

Escaped, bereaved,
The shawled man sits on grass
Holding the Torah in its scarlet coat:

His childhood and his way.
His feet right-angled and collapsed
Like damaged birds.

Crossed, where they fell
Beside him, fiddle and bow:
The last note vibrant still.

And watching, regal,
His full-uddered cow
Keeps earth-bound company.

'THREE PERSONS TAKING A WALK'

(August Macke, 1914)

The girls' two bodies
Fit into each other
Like long spoons.

And he, in silence
And in step with them,
A two-pronged fork,

Is watching as they share
Whispering secrets
That will ignore him quite.

On the slow garden path
They move in almost unison,
Oblivious of the tree.

It bends and echoes
Line and shape,
Aware how orange

Twins her blouse
With the trunk's curve,
Arching them through

To waiting blueness
Wide and cool, a world
Behind a purple wall.

THE HOUR

The wire mesh of trees across the street
Tells of a garden now in winter dark,

An empty kitchen's whiteness underneath
Hangs in a basement as suspended life.

No sound creeps through this Sunday afternoon
When windows can be satisfied with light

In a surburban house. Air sleeps alone.
And somewhere now there are the frozen ones,

The old, the lovers without gestures, bled
And bored with such a day. – As quietness

Loops round and round the room, brushing at fear,
It almost prays, almost implores the desk,

The lamp, the chair, to brandish words inside
Another hour's question and retreat.

ANNOTATIONS

Slowly, without clemency, they come,
Annotations of each thought, each move,
Threading their net across my face.

Though I resent them, dread their onus,
Know the savage mime they can induce,
Something in me condones their code.

Maybe, I see in them my grandmother,
Rooted security and village ways
And read her language in the glass;

Or hope for, fear, the lessening pain,
The final dessication of desire
And the demand: childhood's return?

STOCKTAKING

Three score achieved, secured with pen and ink:
Prescriptions free and half fare on the train,
The pension pennies trickle from the bank.

Reductions now at concerts make you blink
And study price-lists with new eyes again.
Three score achieved, secured with pen and ink.

What else is cheaper? Neither food nor drink
But haircuts, inch by inch the same refrain:
The pension pennies trickle from the bank.

Where up to now you spurned the truth and sank
Years that appeared too many and a stain:
Three score achieved, secured with pen and ink.

True, waistlines will expand and chests will sink
All despite eating fibres, wholefood grain.
The pension pennies trickle from the bank.

And what of passions, hope, the heartbeat lump
Thudding in throat and voice? All still remain.
Three score achieved, secured with pen and ink.
The pension pennies trickle from the bank.

THE SAFETY VALVE

With uneven lipstick
The woman came to me,
Asking for German lessons.

Those were her middle-years:
The time to kill,
Mutilate time,

Time to escape
Mostly from self
Trapped in her echo-house.

She tried to locate
A German forebear,
Discover him in her blood,

To pass and lose
The too familiar crowd
And sacrifice the ordinary day.

She took a job:
Assistant in a baker's shop
And practised easy chat,

And handed me my bread
With twisted breath
Asking for German lessons.

DEATH IN OCTOBER

She carried her sentences like a flag
In speech as explosive as her red dress;
I remember her unexpected grace
At the Christmas dance last year, her zest
When she flung each solid limb to the drum
And beat of the steel-band's tune.

It is autumn now – with a breathlessness
Of scorching leaves in galloping wind:
A last flamboyance before their fall;
But for her, who could not wait any more,
This time was too dense with auburn hurt
As light buried light in her room.

USELESS

While mothers wail, the children starve and die,
The wheat lies useless on the surplus hill
Because there is no gold in their young cry.

Now is the time of beet-smoke in the sky
And blanket-heavy hangs that malted smell
While mothers wail, the children starve and die.

We coddle cats and dogs and wonder why
Some lie spreadeagled in the road, quite still,
Because there is no gold in their young cry.

To save our men from heart disease we try
To follow doctors' anti-butter drill
While mothers wail, the children starve and die.

The cattle vanish as the milk runs dry;
Our dustbins reek with wasted food and spill;
There is no gold in those young children's cry.

The four winds gather substance for each lie,
The spokesmen eat their words against their will
While mothers wail, the children starve and die
Because there is no gold in their young cry.

NON-PERSON

*'Here lies the son of Goethe'**

Had he no name,
How came he to be buried
In this Roman grave,
Was it his father's fame
That bought the plot?

Poor, ordinary August Goethe,
You must have searched and travelled far,
Perhaps to try and find the same
Rebirth and insight as your father did
In Italy, and yet, just over forty,
Dead – no name to show the world
Your own significance.

Sad, doubly so, that you lie here
Where tourists come to honour Keats
And Shelley, stumbling past you.
One of five, you were, the only one
Surviving till they set you up in this
Small patch of Roman earth,
Seen, though unlooked for, now, by accident.

** This is the inscription on the tombstone,
there is no Christian name.*

RELICS

I

In an old shoe-box they wait
For their resurrection: a torch,
Tin plates, a fire-fighter's
Manual, and in a pimply
Oil-cloth cover: the head
Hugging gas-mask. Here it curls
Its dark long snout, naive
Unused monstrosity
In nearly new condition, ready
For someone's brief survival.

II

The young curator views it
With collector's eyes, gives it
A number, writes its pedigree,
And lets the order of the
Catalogue dispense its age,
Its colour, measurements, feed
The computer's belly.

III

Together with new relics
It will rest, this so-called
Saviour of a never-land,
Until a generation
Not yet born, and occupied
With workless days, will stare
At these mementos under
Glass, grin at their ancestors'
Ingenious innocence.

IN A REFERENCE LIBRARY

Under dull 'flora' glass,
With newsprint reverence, they sit

At long refectory tables,
Workless, on a rainy day.

Heads bent in hushed soliloquies
Inside a skin of silence

That shudders only with
Rain-muted wheels outside

When suddenly, dark-bearded, quick,
A man walks down the centre aisle

Playing at priesthood, mumbling
Parables and sermons, to and fro

He marches, pointing fingers
At uneasy looks that turn

Immediately to their own homily:
The murder of the morning.

NEW YEAR'S EVE

We hardly noticed that old knotty tramp
Wolfing his food (a place near Leicester Square)

Until there crossed a steel of voices, rush
Of shoes: 'Two pounds you owe us, you'll not go

Before you've paid!' He rumbled broken words,
Half sentences, tried running to the door

But fists came clamping down to trap him, push
Him to the basement stairs; one final kick,

Threat of police, was all we heard. Cowards,
We were, who sipped the year's last cup of tea

In silent fellow-travellership when faced
With hunger, cruelty, our undone deeds.

III

WEST WALL, LONGTHORPE TOWER

Legend and gesso meet
On this thick wall
With line and pigment
Ready to embalm some history.

The bed stood here
Where Anthony looks down
On one weaving a basket,
While underneath

In pointed dispute stand
Philosopher and pupil
Seeking a unity
To complement each other.

Nearby, a narrow, deep-set
Window forms a seat
For us to rest, to watch the street,
To draw in stripes of light

That paint the limestone
Apricot. Familiar
Herons from the Nene
Wait in unchanging stillness here.

They face the Labours
Of each month
Where every line insists
On busyness
Inside this chamber's quietude.

EASTER SUNDAY

Today, on the North Bank,
Bunches of chickweed
Guard our walk.
Easter Sunday locks
Each footprint
Into clay, stones
Idle where they fall
Under inevitable sky.
A swan stands
On a black field's edge,
A domino dot
In the drama of solitude.
A dog barks his caution
As we pass by,
Wind-washed,
Free from speech.

AUGUST GARDEN

Sun-warm the early berries bleed my hands,
The smells of summer emphasise the air
And apples start to fall in ones and twos.

A sunflower alone stands taller than the fence,
The harnessed lifeline through its hairy stem
Projects a face, a dark-brown velvet disk

Alive with bees inside a yellow fringe.
Turned hungry to the sun it echoes strength:
A weather-gleam proclaims its yearly yes.

SPECULATION ABOUT A EUCALYPTUS TREE

Looking at the Eucalyptus tree
In my neighbour's garden,
I smell the hot oil of Australia
But see the cool wind of Europe
Brushing its leaves.

Descendant of exiled ancestors,
The tree has grown healthy and tall.
I wonder, if in its white trunk
And slate-blue leaves there moves
A different dawn,

Or if different seasons
Still waken in years
Of unexplained strangeness,
Like forgotten half-sisters,
Under a neutral sun?

PAVEMENT CAFE

Outside the girl with long red hair
Talks to her man.
She spreads her hands to emphasize
A point, and lets
Her fingers drop like dying swans.

He listens, sips his coffee, smokes,
While still she pours
The rhythm of her talk through wrists
And fingertips,
Intently now, as pointed rock.

There is no answer in his pose.
No counterpoint.
Only the turning of the eyes.
The noonday heat
Sweats on his body, his bored skin.

CLIMBING

There is no falseness
Up, in the mountains,

Your breath is needed
For the truth of climbing

Each step a muscle
Of life, achieved,

Words are not acceptable
Where glaciers lie

In their yearly retreating
On the rough bank of rock

Under funeral clouds
Or exploding sun,

Even love is banished
While your body belongs

To thinning air,
And you envy the crows'

Effortless circling
Of the sky's harbour.

MATTMARK, Switzerland

The air, thin tissue razored white,
Wraps up this dam, this milky green
That curls from shore to shore. Birds cut

Their angles to the rocks and each
Small plant must prove its tough resilience
To the wind. The sun is bleaching

Grass like hair. Hard, out of stone, like
Diamonds, men's faces stare at us
Their early deaths: all makers

Of this place. False flowers fringe their names.
The waters, peerless, foam and shout
Their glacier song. The switch of power waits.

TWO INCIDENTS

As we approach, a dumb tumult
Of angry trout shoots to the edge

Of the mountain lake: oblivious of fear,
Quick-shimmering under mute rings

They crowd like cross-stitch over each other
Snapping at non-existent food.

On the way down, steam rising
From a zinc bath at the roadside farm:

A whole family bending over it,
A coloured oval of shaking behinds,

Their arms scraping zigzag patterns
On the white belly of a killed pig.

Even the toddler is busy watching
With glee, no trace of fear or pity.

We, fresh from city pavements,
Stand still in acute amazement,

Face to face, for the second time
That morning, with the heat of hunger.

ONCE

Once, when colour of hope
Shone sunflower-tall,
No fear of dawn shook day.

Light was the root of time
Opening life on life.
Death is too short a word

For this grey falling.

WINTER APPEASEMENT

In a room,
After the first light is lit,
Two people.

Outside
The snow has died
Leaving rain

On the road:
Wet mirrors of lamplight
And winter Dark

Reach for
The woman crossing the room
By the window;

She moves
In her own rhythm, her doubt
Bruising the silence,

Rehearsing
The ghosts of her winter
Appeasement.

UNRIPE THOUGHTS

They must have planned
Their fierce campaign, those birds

That pecked and knocked
The apples till they dropped,

Still white-pipped, green
And full of acid juice.

Defenceless weights,
We had to pick them then,

A weak retreat,
A human subterfuge

To cosset them
Like unripe thoughts, store them

In darkness, cool,
Each a wrapped future hope.

QUINCES

One year
The quinces hung like lanterns
From the tree,
Their amber sweetness harvesting
A light
That glows and trembles through
The jars;
The jelly set in slithering
Rounds of glass
Hoarding the taste of autumn's
Heavy gold,
Melting the ice of winter
From our tongues.

NOVEMBER

After the words the wind
Crashes round the house
Fisting the bricks,

The eaves ache under the roof
Crying out to the trees
In their cousinship,

The night arrives in a dark sheet
Calling the day's tumult
To a vesper of sleep

In this menopause of the year,
This auburn change of tired leaves
When light turns inward.

CORMORANT AT BRIGHTON MARINA

The huge bird roots himself
On a plank of wood
Flapping his dragon wings.

He is a separate dream
Among resting ships
Telling no one his nightmares.

We walk here, under cliffs,
At the year's ending
Feeding on sun and wind,

Startle to see him there again:
A greedy question mark,
The black ghost of a wave,

In this cocoon maze of the sea.

NIGHT DRIVE

Tonight in the frost
Trees are silver coral
That curves and clusters
In a black sea.

You drive through
Silent waves of lanes
Like wandering fish
From home to home.

WORDS

Words tell me to iron out seconds,
To pepper the precis of years.

In one small cobweb they touch
Fragrance and method of thought.

Call it a wound or a serpent's voice
Bleeding sounds at the nerves' barricade,

The sister spider of evening
Waiting under the day's bandage.

IV
VERSIONS

WILL-O'-THE-WISPS

(after Rainer Maria Rilke)

We commune in old established ways
with the lights in the fen.
They seem like great-aunts to me . . . and then
I discover between us

more and more that family trait
no power can suppress:
this swing, this leap, this jerk, this flight,
others try it without success.

I too am there where the roads will end
In marsh-grass many have shunned,
and often I've seen myself snuffed out
under the eyelid's hand.

THE BACHELOR

(after Rilke)

Lamplight on abandoned papers and the night
surrounding all far into the wooden
cupboards. And it happened that he might
lose himself, melt with his own kind;
the more he read, it seemed to him he had their pride
yet all of them had his in their possession.

With arrogance the empty chairs were stiffening
along the wall, and only self-indulgent feelings
were spreading sleep among the furniture;
from high above the night was pouring itself down
onto the pendulum, and trembling from its golden
mill, his time ran very finely ground.

He did not take it. To go amongst them
feverishly as if to tear away their bodies'
shrouds, grab at those other times.
Until his whispering (what distanced him?)
He praised one of those letter writers
as if the letter were for him: you know me most
of all; and cheerfully he tapped the chair's two arms.
But then the mirror, in inner liberty,
let go a curtain, then a window, silently:
because there stood, almost complete, the ghost.

THE INSANE ONES

(after Rilke)

And they're silent, for the wall-partitions
have been taken from their minds,
and the hours when we'd understand them
heave and start and fade from sight.

When at night they're stepping to the window:
suddenly all life is good.
In the concrete world their hands are staying,
and the heart is tall and could be praying,
and the eyes with rested look

see the often changing unexpected
garden, peaceful in its ordered life,
there, where foreign worlds remain reflected
still it grows, never to lose itself.

YOU KNOW, THOSE CLOUDS
SHAPED FROM THAT OPEN GREY

You know, those clouds shaped from that open grey
revealing chambers through their endless spaces,
where higher even than a bird can stray
star visions walk since myriad years and paces,
that now and then will touch us through a grey
from which we surface: wonderfully plied
with distant confluence. Sometimes attracted by
the stubborness of earth, sometimes a light
(a sudden) all-engulfing by entire worlds . . .

RAINER MARIA RILKE

77

SONG

(after Rainer Maria Rilke)

You, whom I will not tell that at night
I lie weeping,
whose being is my fatiguing fight,
my cradled keeping,
you, who tells nothing of the wide
waking for me:
should we carry this light
in us silently
never to be stilled?

Look at the lovers, how soon
after their knowing began
they lie and are spilled.

You isolate me. Only in you is my replacing.
For a while it is you, then again it is the rustling,
or it is a fragrance without dust.
Ah, in my arms I have lost every love I have worn,
but you, only you are constantly reborn:
because I never quite held you, I hold you fast.

SKY MOURNING

(after Nikolaus Lenau)

Across the face of sky a thought is walking,
That gloomy cloud up there, heavy with fear;
As on his bed a man suffering in spirit
The wind-tossed shrub is twisting to and fro.

The sky intones faint, melancholy rumbling
Blinking its dusky eyelash now and then,
– as eyes are blinking when intent on weeping –
And from the eyelash flickers feeble gleam.

Now from the marshland slither cooling showers
And silent mist across the heath and fen;
The sky, still musing on its mournful sorrow,
Lets lazily the sun fall from its hand.

BOTH

(after Hugo von Hofmannsthal)

She held the chalice in her hand
– Her chin and mouth echoed its rim –
So light and certain was her step
She did not spill a single drop.

So light and steady was his hand
As he was riding his young horse
And with an easy gesture forced
It to a halt and, trembling, stand.

But when he should have, from her hand,
Taken the chalice, light and round,
Its weight for both was much too great
Because they both were shaking so
That not one hand the other found
And dark-red wine rolled on the ground.